"Children want heroes. Christian biographies offer up true stories that invite children to see the greatness of God's power at work through his people."
MELISSA KRUGER, Author; Director of Women's Initiatives, The Gospel Coalition

"This is a wonderful book. I'm going to give copies to as many families as I can."
SUSAN SUTTON, International Director, WEC International

"This little book about my dear friend and missionary colleague Dr Helen is so well written and illustrated that it should inspire many children of this generation to want to serve God too."
MAUD KELLS, Missionary in DR Congo

"A wonderful story of perseverance that I will read to my children over and over again!"
COURTNEY REISSIG, Author, *Teach Me to Feel*

"Inspiring, challenging, heartwarming and true! This will touch the hearts of young and old alike."
LINDA ALLCOCK, Author, *Head, Heart, Hands* and *Deeper Still*

"I love this book! It left me deeply moved and hugely encouraged!"
ANDREA TREVENNA, Associate Minister for Women, St Nicholas Church, Sevenoaks

"Helen Roseveare's life still speaks. Her real story will help children see their real need for Jesus."
BARBARA REAOCH, Author, *A Jesus Christmas* and *A Jesus Easter*

"Helen speaks to us today through her inspirational life, poured out in worship, love and selfless service to her great Master, the Lord Jesus Christ."
PAT MORTON, Long-time friend of Helen Roseveare

"I would love to think that this powerful story of faith, sacrifice, courage and perseverance would inspire another generation of children to give their lives in the service of Jesus."
BOB HARTMAN, Author, *The Prisoners, the Earthquake, and the Midnight Song*

Helen Roseveare
© Laura Caputo-Wickham 2023. Reprinted 2023.

Illustrated by Cecilia Messina | Design and Art Direction by André Parker
Photograph on page 24 courtesy of Christian Focus
"The Good Book For Children" is an imprint of The Good Book Company Ltd.
thegoodbook.com | thegoodbook.co.uk | thegoodbook.com.au
thegoodbook.co.nz | thegoodbook.co.in
ISBN: 9781784987466 | JOB-007583 | Printed in India

thegoodbook
for children

Helen Roseveare

The Doctor Who Kept Going No Matter What

Laura Caputo-Wickham

Illustrated by Cecilia Messina

On the day of her eighth birthday, Helen sat in Sunday school cutting and sticking pictures of far-away countries and, in her heart, made a decision:

"When I grow up, I will travel the world and tell other boys and girls about Jesus."

And, being the determined girl that she was, Helen's mind was made up once and for all.

When she started university to become a doctor,
Helen worried.

She worried she wouldn't make any friends.
She worried she wouldn't do well with her exams.
She worried she didn't really know God after all.

Then, one evening, Helen looked up and found a
Bible verse written on a wall:

BE STILL, AND KNOW THAT I AM GOD.

PSALM 46 v 10

At once, Helen knew that God was with her.
And a big sense of peace and stillness filled
her worried heart.

After finishing university, Helen went to missionary-training school, where she spent her time studying the Bible and wondering where in the world God would send her.

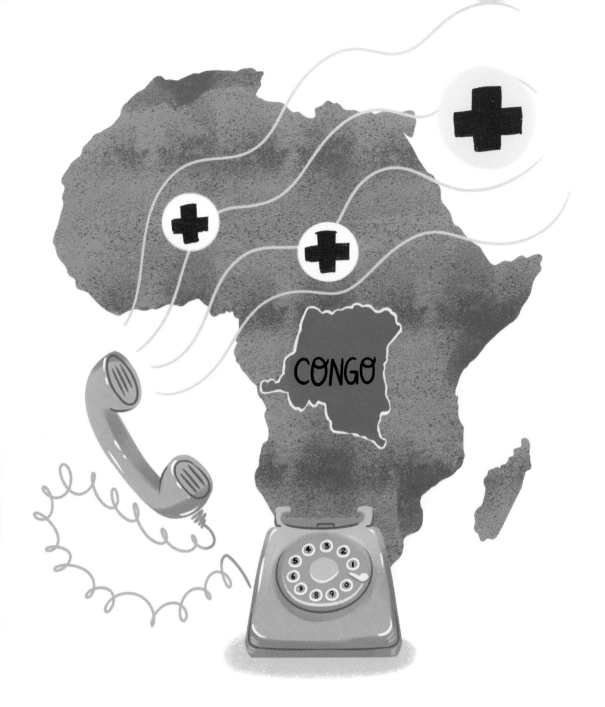

Then, one day, the missionary school received a call for help from Congo, a big country in the centre of Africa.
"We need more doctors!"
Thankfully, they had the perfect person for the job!

Helen set off on a long journey that took her to the heart of Africa, and, once there, she worked non-stop.

She helped build the hospital,
looked after the patients,
trained new doctors and nurses...

... and read the Bible with many
people, telling them how they
could trust Jesus as their King.

Just like the mountains that surrounded her,
Helen's life had many ups and many downs.

Good times when she joined her friends,
singing and dancing for Jesus...

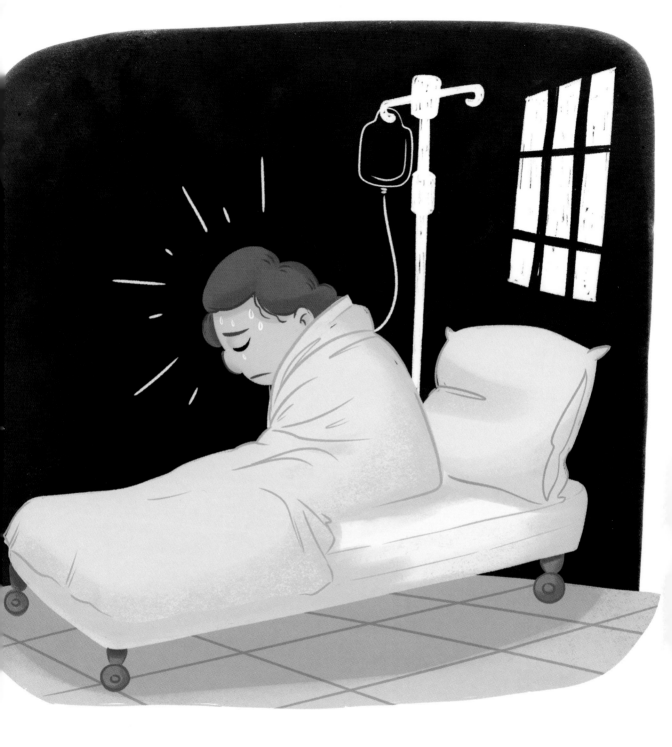

... and bad times when she was the one needing a doctor!

One night, Helen helped a woman give birth to a baby.

"The baby needs to stay warm," she told the nurses, "or else he might die!"

But there were no hot-water bottles, so it was
difficult to keep the baby warm.

Helen was worried.

The nurses were worried.
The baby's big sister was worried too.

When Helen asked some of the children she cared for to pray for the baby, a girl named Ruth closed her eyes.

"Please, God," she prayed, "send us a water bottle. It'll be no good tomorrow, so please send it this afternoon." She then added, "Send a doll too, for the baby's big sister, so she'll know that you love her".

That very afternoon, Helen received a big box from England. Helen had never received a parcel before.

Inside, she found a hot-water bottle...

and a doll.

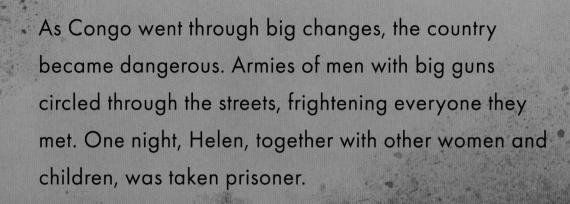

As Congo went through big changes, the country became dangerous. Armies of men with big guns circled through the streets, frightening everyone they met. One night, Helen, together with other women and children, was taken prisoner.

For five dreadful months Helen went through
a lot of suffering.

But through it all, she remembered that God had
said, "Be still, and know that I am God" — and
that same sense of peace, which she had felt many
times before, returned stronger than ever.

Then, one day, a loud noise made Helen peep outside her prison window. She saw jeeps, trucks and many soldiers.

"Help is here!" she breathed.
The terrible nightmare was finally over.

Safe and sound, Helen travelled back
to England...
but only for a little while...

... because, as soon as it was safe to do so, she returned to Congo...

... picking up right from where she had left off.

Helen Roseveare

1925 – 2016

"Be still, and know that I am God."

Psalm 46 v 10

Questions to Think About

1. Which part of Helen's story did you like best?

2. Do you remember how God answered Helen and Ruth's prayer for a hot-water bottle and a doll? Do you know someone who needs God's help? What could you pray for them now?

3. Helen used her many gifts to serve God, including as a doctor in Congo and as an author who wrote many books. What gifts has God given you? How could you use one of them to serve God this week?

4. What ideas does Helen's story give you about how you might serve Jesus when you are older?

5. What is one truth about God that you'd like to remember from this story?

Helen Roseveare

21 September 1925 Helen was born in Hertfordshire, England to Sir Martin and Lady Edith Roseveare. She was the second of five children. Her father was a mathematician who designed the ration books used in the UK during the Second World War.

July 1944 Helen went to Newnham College in Cambridge, England to study to become a doctor.
As well as studying, Helen also played hockey for the university's team and joined a group of students who met regularly to read the Bible. During these Bible studies, Helen got to know Jesus better and truly fell in love with him, as she liked to describe it.

15th January 1951 After finishing university, Helen moved to the headquarters of WEC (Worldwide Evangelisation for Christ), where she trained to become a missionary.

13th February 1953 Helen embarked on a long journey that took her to what used to be called the Belgian Congo. Since then, Congo has had different names and is today known as the Democratic Republic of the Congo. There, Helen helped set up hospitals and trained nurses and doctors.

30th June 1960 Congo declared independence from Belgium, and a long period of unrest followed.

In 1964, Helen was taken prisoner by a group of rebel soldiers who treated her very badly.
Five months later, Helen was freed, and she returned safely to England.

11th March 1966 After two years of rest in the UK, Helen returned to Congo, where she served for seven more years.

7th December 2016 Helen died at the age of 91 after having spent her last years sharing her story through rousing talks and life-changing books. Many people are still encouraged and inspired by her powerful testimony.

NORTH
AMERICA

EU

United
Kingdom

SOUTH
AMERICA

World Map

Where in the world
did Helen's story
take place?

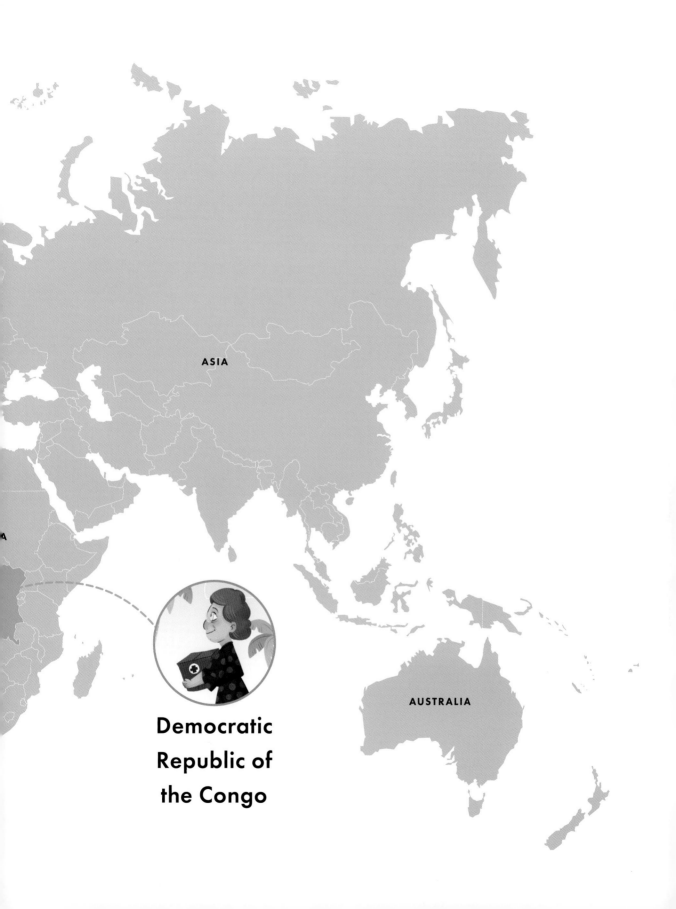

ASIA

AUSTRALIA

Democratic
Republic of
the Congo

Interact with Helen's Story!

_____'s

Family Project: Congo

Helen Roseveare became a missionary to Congo* in 1953 when she was 28 years old. As you learn about the people of Congo, take time to pray for the Christians there and the people who don't yet know about Jesus! Read and discuss Matthew 28 v 16–20 and Revelation 7 v 9–11 together to learn about God's heart for all peoples.

Day 1: Overview

- Locate Congo on a globe or map.
- How many people live in Congo?

_____

- Look up pictures of Congo.

Day 2: Food

- What is a typical meal in Congo?

_____

- What sort of meals might Helen have eaten in Congo?

_____

- What are some popular snacks?

_____

- If you can, make a Congolese meal together.

*The region has sometimes been one country, and other times two. It has had many different names. To keep it simple, we call the region Helen served in "Congo."

1

Day 3: Culture

- What are some of the holidays celebrated in Congo?

_____

- Read an overview of the history of Congo.
- What makes up traditional Congolese clothing?

Toys & Games

- What sort of toys are popular in Congo?

_____

- What games do children in Congo like to play?

_____

- What is school like in Congo?

_____

Day 5: Religion & Missions

- What are the primary religions in Congo?

_____

- How many Christians are in Congo?

_____

- Are there any unreached people groups in Congo?

_____

- What are church services like in Congo?

_____

All About
Helen Roseveare

4-7s

By: _____

My Drawing of Helen Roseveare

Where did Helen go to school?
_____
_____

When was Helen born?
_____

How old was Helen when she decided to be a missionary?
_____

What Did Helen Do When...

Circle the Answer

She was worried at university — Saw a Bible verse on the wall OR Kept worrying

She went to Congo — Made balloon animals OR Helped as a doctor

She needed a water bottle — Prayed with Ruth OR Made her own water bottle

She got freed from prison — Went to a new country OR Went back to Congo

1

Biography Report for
Helen Roseveare

8-11s

By: _____

My favorite thing about Helen:
_____
_____

Person from the Bible Helen reminds me of:
_____
_____

A question I would ask Helen:
_____
_____

Three words I would use to describe Helen:
1. _____
2. _____
3. _____

Remember this Verse Helen Loved

"Be _____ and _____ that
_____ am _____ ."
Psalm 46 v 10

Can you say it 5 times without looking?

1

Helen Ro...
Year of ...

Hom...

Search Online to Find:
Ask an adult about doing this together!

What books did Helen write?

What was the name of the hospital Helen worked at?

What kinds of work does Worldwide Evangelisation for Christ do today?

Download Free Resources at
thegoodbook.com/kids-resources

Do Great Things for God

Inspiring Biographies for Young Children

Corrie ten Boom
The Courageous Woman and the Secret Room
Laura Caputo-Wickham
Illustrated by Isabel Muñoz

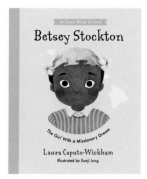

Betsey Stockton
The Girl With a Missionary Dream
Laura Caputo-Wickham
Illustrated by Eunji Jung

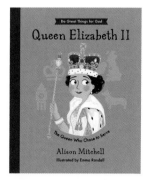

Queen Elizabeth II
The Queen Who Chose to Serve
Alison Mitchell
Illustrated by Emma Randall

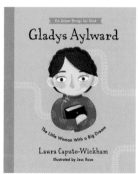

Gladys Aylward
The Little Woman With a Big Dream
Laura Caputo-Wickham
Illustrated by Jess Rose

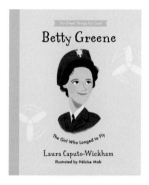

Betty Greene
The Girl Who Longed to Fly
Laura Caputo-Wickham
Illustrated by Hélaïse Mab

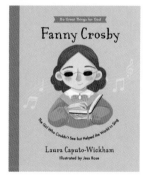

Fanny Crosby
The Girl Who Couldn't See but Helped the World to Sing
Laura Caputo-Wickham
Illustrated by Jess Rose

Maria Fearing
The Girl Who Dreamed of Distant Lands
K. A. Ellis
Illustrated by Isabel Muñoz

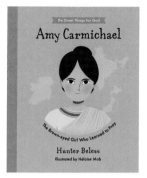

Amy Carmichael
The Brown-eyed Girl Who Learned to Pray
Hunter Beless
Illustrated by Hélaïse Mab

Helen Roseveare
The Doctor Who Kept Going No Matter What
Laura Caputo-Wickham
Illustrated by Cecilia Messina

thegoodbook.com | thegoodbook.co.uk